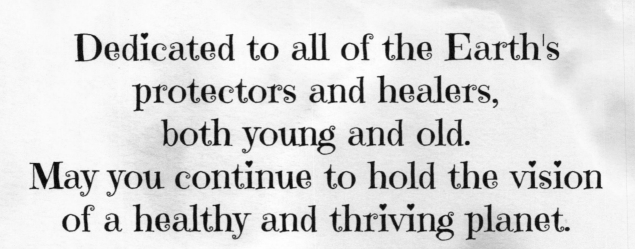

Dedicated to all of the Earth's
protectors and healers,
both young and old.
May you continue to hold the vision
of a healthy and thriving planet.

Text and illustrations © Rachael Rose Zoller 2017
Printed by createspace
Available from Amazon.com & other retail outlets
First Edition.

PROTECT
The Pollinators

Written & Illustrated by
Rachael Rose Zoller

Throughout all of the Earth's
jungles and deserts,
across all forests,
meadows and fields...

You will find special creatures called
"Pollinators"

Pollinators are the birds, bees, butterflies, bugs and bats

and other insects and mammals that deposit pollen into a plant.

What is pollen?
If you'd like to know, pollen helps fruit and
seed to grow!

Berries, banana,
papaya, peas and plum,
oranges, avocado...

Can you think of some?

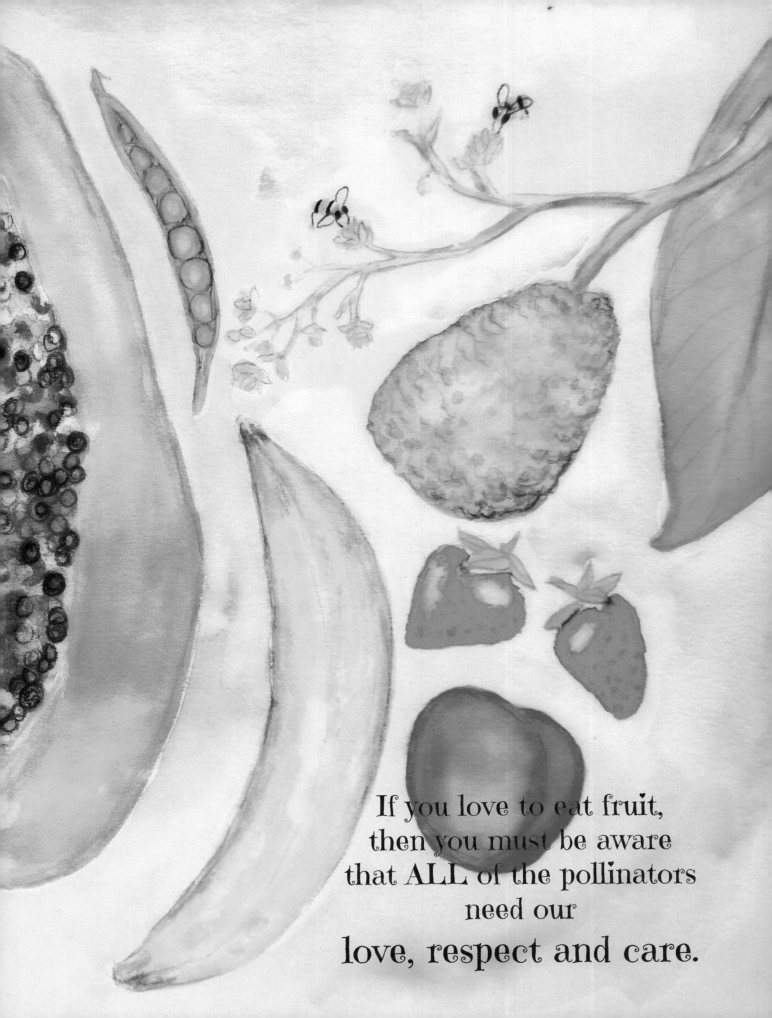

If you love to eat fruit,
then you must be aware
that ALL of the pollinators
need our
love, respect and care.

By planting flowers and
choosing organic,
we can protect the pollinators
all over the planet!

So come along and you will see
some of the Earth's many
pollinators,
let's start with the...

Bee!

Bees love to buzz all day in the sun
as they move from stamen to flower.

Bees visit thousands of flowers each day,
eating nectar and collecting pollen
along the way.

If a bee lands on you, don't be afraid...
Just say "Hello!" and gently guide them away.

In Costa Rica, what a beautiful sight!
A Blue Morpho Butterfly,
so BIG and so BRIGHT!

These Blue Morphos are graceful
as they glide through the air,
softly pollinating tropical flowers
everywhere.

The Chocolate Midge is so tiny and cute.
She is the only insect that pollinates the
sacred cacao fruit.

Cacao, once processed, turns into
chocolate.
Thank you, Chocolate Midge!

In the American South West,
where the cactus flowers bloom,
bats love to pollinate them
underneath the moon!

The bright orange Monarch Butterfly
migrates from the rain forests of Mexico,
over the mountains of California and on to
Canada for the spring.

They stop to snack on the nectar
of brightly colored flowers
and pollinate on their long journey.

Have you ever heard the humming
of the Hummingbird?
Have you seen them ZOOM and DANCE
through the air while in flight?

Then they fly down
to kiss the flowers
and sip the sweet nectar
with delight.

The Earth is filled with
many wonderful pollinators;

There are:
butterflies,
lizards,
moths,
birds,
ants and bugs
of all kinds.

Last we will visit
a very LARGE pollinator.

Not a bat,
not a bird, or a bee...

This big, furry, black and white
mammal builds nests in the tree
tops and swings from the branches
of trees!

Can you guess who this creature
might be?

The Black and White Ruffed Lemur eats
nectar from blossoms and pollinates the
Traveler's Tree.

Now that you have learned about seven of the Earth's pollinators, you see that they are very special indeed.

To protect the pollinators, all we must do is give them safe space to thrive and be free.

The End.

10 Ways To Protect Pollinators Near You:

1. Plant an organic, pollinator garden!
2. Never use toxic chemical pesticides.
3. When purchasing plants, make sure they were not treated with "Neonicotinoids"
4. Avoid red dye for hummingbird water, only use real sugar and water.
5. Plant native plants in your garden for pollinators to enjoy.
6. Support your local, organic farmers.
7. Look for foods with the "non-gmo" label.
8. Build a DIY pollinator nesting habitat.
9. Spread the awareness on the importance of keeping pollinators safe.
10. Visit www.rachaelrosezoller.com/protectthepollinators for more tips, crafts, DIYs and other pollinator friendly resources!

Pollinator Friendly Websites & Resources:

www.nongmoproject.org
"The Non-GMO Project is a nonprofit organization committed to preserving and building sources of non-GMO products, educating consumers and providing verified non-GMO choices."

www.projectpollinate.org
"Project Pollinate is an educational and research organization dedicated to informing communities about the interconnectedness of our ecosystem while providing habitats and sanctuary for honeybees, native bees and other pollinators..."

www.thegoodofthehive.com
"Artist Matthew Willey is the founder of The Good of the Hive Initiative, and has committed to personally paint 50,000 honeybees – the number necessary for a healthy, thriving hive – in murals around the world. Through art and imagination, The Good of the Hive raises awareness about the current struggle and population decline of honeybees while celebrating their incredible behaviors."

www.beedowntown.org
"Our innovative approach uses cities, and the businesses in them, to collaboratively rebuild healthy honey bee populations. We install and maintain groups of beehives, sponsored by local businesses, at landmark locations in urban areas"

www.rareseeds.com
"Buy Heirloom Garden Seeds online. Over 1800 varieties of Vegetables, Rare Flowers & Herbs. 100% Non-GMO open pollinated seeds."

www.goldenbee.com.au
"Golden Bee is a global collective of creative collaborators inspired by literal and metaphoric engagement with bees. At the heart of the project are notions of interconnection, sustainability in all spheres, and the linking of art, ideas and community to further social and cultural progress."

www.panna.org
"At Pesticide Action Network (PAN) North America, we work to create a just, thriving food system... PAN works with those on the frontlines to tackle the pesticide problem — and reclaim the future of food and farming...."

www.pollinatorsnativeplants.com
"A comprehensive guide illustrating the bees that occur in north-central and eastern United States and southern Canada."

CPSIA information can be obtained
at www.ICGtesting.com
Printed in the USA
LVHW071753060521
686700LV00001B/49